DINOSAURS 3D
AN INCREDIBLE JOURNEY THROUGH TIME

Dougal Dixon

TIME
FOR KIDS

TIME Home Entertainment
Publisher Jim Childs
Vice President, Brand & Digital Strategy Steven Sandonato
Executive Director, Marketing Services Carol Pittard
Executive Director, Retail & Special Sales Tom Mifsud
Executive Publishing Director Joy Butts
Director, Bookazine Development & Marketing Laura Adam
Finance Director Glenn Buonocore
Associate Publishing Director Megan Pearlman
Assistant General Counsel Helen Wan
Assistant Director, Special Sales Ilene Schreider
Senior Book Production Manager Susan Chodakiewicz
Design & Prepress Manager Anne-Michelle Gallero
Brand Manager Jonathan White
Associate Prepress Manager Alex Voznesenskiy
Associate Production Manager Kimberly Marshall
Assistant Brand Manager Stephanie Braga

Editorial Director Stephen Koepp
TIME For Kids
Managing Editor Nellie Gonzalez Cutler
Editor, Time Learning Ventures Jonathan Rosenbloom

Created for TIME For Kids by **Bender Richardson White**
Publisher: Kim Richardson
Editorial Director: Lionel Bender
Design Director and Picture Researcher: Ben White
Digital Conversion: Neil Sutton
Proofreader: Laura Booth
Illustrators: Sebastian Quigley, Sam Weston

Special thanks: Katherine Barnet, Jeremy Biloon, Rose Cirrincione, Jacqueline Fitzgerald, Christine Font, Jenna Goldberg, Hillary Hirsch, David Kahn, Amy Mangus, Amy Migliaccio, Nina Mistry, Dave Rozzelle, Ricardo Santiago, Adriana Tierno, Vanessa Wu

For information on TIME For Kids magazine for the classroom or home, go to TIMEFORKIDS.COM or call 1-800-777-8600.
For subscriptions to SI Kids, go to SIKIDS.COM or call 1-800-889-6007.

Published by TIME For Kids Books,
An imprint of Time Home Entertainment Inc.
135 West 50th Street
New York, NY 10020

ISBN 10: 1-61893-044-3
ISBN 13: 978-1-61893-044-6
Library of Congress Control Number: 2013932158

TIME For Kids is a trademark of Time Inc.

We welcome your comments and suggestions about TIME For KidsBooks. Please write to us at:
TIME For Kids Books, Attention: Book Editors, P.O. Box 11016, Des Moines, IA 50336-1016
If you would like to order any of our hardcover Collector's Edition books, please call us at 1-800-327-6388 (Monday through Friday, 7 a.m. to 8 p.m., or Saturday, 7 a.m. to 6 p.m., Central Time).

1 TLF 13

CONTENTS

MEET THE DINOSAURS

DINOSAUR TIMES

MEAT-EATERS

LONG-NECKED PLANT-EATERS

ARMORED, PLATED AND HORNED

TWO-FOOTED PLANT-EATERS

DIGGING UP THE PAST

ABOUT THIS BOOK

Dinosaurs 3D takes you back more than 65 million years to a time when our planet was a very different place and dinosaurs ruled the land. You'll discover some of the most amazing and unusual dinosaurs and learn how they lived. Photos of modern animals connect how they live today with how dinosaurs lived long ago. Using 3D-illustrations the book brings dinosaurs to life. So get ready, get set to travel back in time as you enter the fascinating world of dinosaurs, some of the most awesome creatures that ever lived.

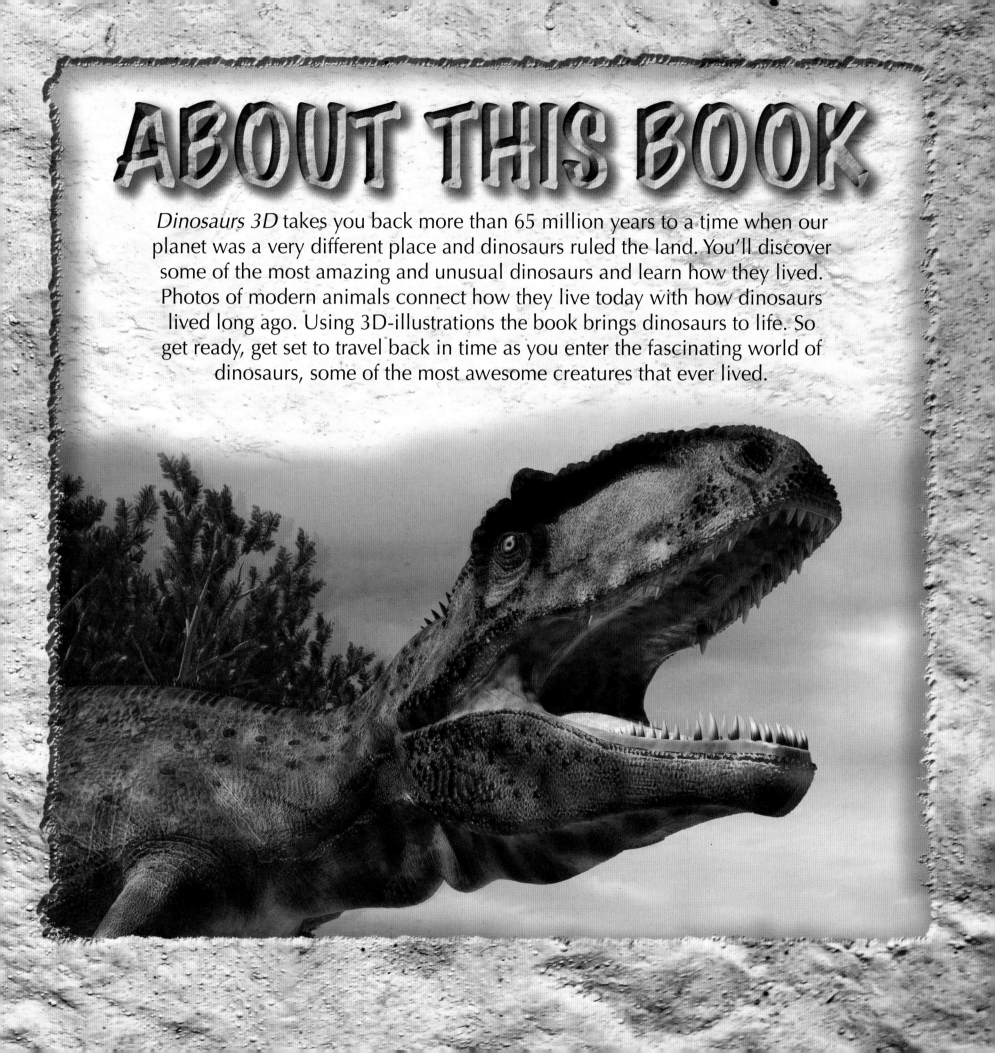

INCREDIBLE CREATURES

When dinosaurs ruled planet Earth

MILLIONS OF YEARS AGO

In fact files throughout the book, "million years ago" is shortened to "mya."

Animals as big as houses moving slowly through a forest, eating all the leaves as they go. Fearsome monsters with giant teeth and claws, capable of killing and eating any animal around. Creatures such as these actually existed, way back in time.

PICTURING THE PAST

On Earth some 225 million years ago, the land and seas were in different positions than they are today. Climates were different and living things were different, too. Dinosaurs ruled the animal world. There were no flowering plants, no birds and no big mammals. From fossil evidence we can imagine what the living world was like long ago.

A skeleton of the fearsome *Tyrannosaurus* can be built from its fossil bones.

DINOSAUR BONES

From fossil dinosaur bones scientists have recreated these prehistoric animals.
By studying dinosaur skeletons in museums it is possible to build up pictures of how these creatures lived and died.

The word "dinosaur" comes from Greek words and means "terrible lizard." This huge meat-eating dinosaur, *Tyrannosaurus*, must have been terrible and, like all other dinosaurs, it was built somewhat like a lizard, a modern reptile, and lived like one.

A meat-eater, a *Ceratosaurus*, attacks an armored plant-eater, a *Stegosaurus*. Behind them scuttle *Dysalotosaurus*, small, two-legged plant-eaters, and a herd of *Brachiosaurus*— long-necked plant-eaters.

TYPES OF DINOSAURS
Dinosaurs came in different shapes, sizes and types

Scientists have found the remains of more than 500 different kinds of dinosaurs.

THE FIERCE ONES

Meat-eaters were fierce. They had long jaws with big teeth and small bodies. They walked on strong hind legs, balanced by a heavy tail. Among the plant-eating dinosaurs, some were huge, had long necks and tails and walked on all fours. Some were small and went about on their back legs. Others were covered in plates of armor and had big horns and walked on all fours. Like today, there were more types of plant-eaters than meat-eaters. This was because there was a rich plant life, including high trees, low-growing ferns and medium-sized bushes.

MEAT-EATERS

LONG-NECKED PLANT-EATERS

ARMORED, PLATED AND HORNED

TWO-FOOTED PLANT-EATERS

THE FOUR MAIN GROUPS OF DINOSAUR

In this book dinosaurs are divided into four main groups—meat-eaters and three types of plant-eaters. Experts know how dinosaurs looked and lived based on clues and evidence buried in rocks. As scientists learn new information or interpret fossil finds in new ways, descriptions of dinosaurs will change, too.

MEET A MEAT-EATER

Fossils tell us a lot about a dinosaur's body

TAIL MUSCLES AND TENDONS
How some fossil bones are linked shows a tail that was stiff and straight or one that was flexible.

Fossils are the remains of once-living plants and animals that have turned to rock.

LIKE MODERN ANIMALS

Scientists know a great deal about the anatomy, or structure, of living animals. By comparing dinosaur fossils to the parts of modern animals, they can build up a detailed picture of dinosaur bodies.

The inside parts of a dinosaur such as its muscles, heart, stomach and brain would have been soft and squishy and they would have rotted away long ago. Marks on fossil dinosaur bones show how muscles were attached and how the bones moved. Imprints in rock reveal dinosaur skin, feathers or eggshell, and hollows among bones highlight the shape and size of soft body parts. The cutaway illustration opposite of a two-legged, meat-eating dinosaur shows how scientists believe its skeleton was built and supported the soft parts.

HIP BONES
The meat-eaters and the long-necked plant-eaters had hip bones arranged like those of a modern reptile. All other dinosaurs had hip bones like those of a modern bird.

LEG MUSCLES
The leg muscles would have been big and strong to carry a very heavy animal.

TENDONS
Usually the toes or the fingers were worked by tendons—strong cables—that were pulled by muscles farther up the leg. Fossil bones often show where the tendons were attached.

DIGESTIVE, OR FOOD-PROCESSING, SYSTEM
These soft parts did not not fossilize. However, a modern plant-eating animal needs a big digestive system to break down its food. This animal appears to have had a small digestive system, supporting other evidence that it was a meat-eater.

SKIN
Dinosaur skin was pebbly like a lizard's or leathery and studded like a crocodile's or covered in featherlike structures like a bird's.

Dinosaur skin

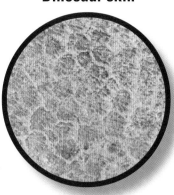

TEETH
Meat-eaters had teeth like steak knives for shearing meat.

Dinosaur teeth

BLOOD SYSTEM
Scientists have found a lump of stone in one dinosaur skeleton that may be a fossilized heart. But this does not reveal if the heart was like that of a reptile, bird or mammal.

CLAWS
Meat-eaters' claws would have had sharp, horny talons for killing. A heavy animal would have had horny hoofs on its toes to support its weight.

FACTS AND GUESSWORK

The most common dinosaur fossils are of bones, teeth and impressions of skin. There are no definite clues for a dinosaur's heart and blood circulation system, its respiratory or breathing system, or its liver, kidneys or eyes. The sizes and weights for dinosaurs given in this book are scientists' best guesses.

Dinosaur bones

A meat-eater, an *Herrerasaurus*, raids the nest of medium-sized plant-eaters, *Riojasaurus*.

Discovering how extinct animals lived makes a dinosaur almost come alive.

TRACE FOSSILS

Dinosaur bones and teeth are "body fossils"—they are the remains of actual parts of an animal. "Trace fossils" show where parts of an animal once were. They include fossil footprints, skin impressions and animal droppings. Fossil dinosaur footprints show if the animals moved alone or in herds and at what speed they moved. Fossil dinosaur droppings provide clues about the animal's food and the structure of its digestive system.

The most exciting dinosaur trace fossils are preserved eggs. They show that dinosaurs built their nests and probably looked after their young as modern birds do.

Studying trace fossils of plants has allowed scientists to build up pictures of the habitats, or natural homes, of dinosaurs. The habitats were as varied as they are in today's natural world—deserts, forests, rivers, seashores.

FOSSIL EGG EVIDENCE

Fossils show that dinosaur eggs were hard-shelled like those of birds and not leathery like those of other reptiles. Scientists have found the bones of unhatched infants inside fossil dinosaur eggs and have imagined how these babies grew.

DINOSAUR SENSES

Hearing
Bones in dinosaurs' ears show that the animals could hear footsteps and one another's calls but not noises such as bird songs.

Eyesight
Some meat-eating dinosaurs such as *Tyrannosaurus* had eyes that pointed forward, allowing them to judge distances while attacking.

Taste and Touch
Dinosaurs seem to have eaten any plant or meat so did not worry about the taste of food. There are no clues about dinosaurs' sense of touch.

Smell
The insides of some dinosaur skulls show complicated bone structures inside their noses. This suggests that dinosaurs had a good sense of smell.

Geology—the study of rocks—shows that Earth and life on it have long histories. It also shows that dinosaurs lived millions of years before humans first appeared.

GOING BACK IN TIME

Planet Earth is more than 4.5 billion years old. Scientists think that there has been life on Earth ever since the planet was solid and cool enough for living things to survive. That is about 3.5 billion years. The first living things would have been tiny bits of living chemical. It was only about 600 million years ago that living things became more complex and started to develop into the variety of plants and animals we see today. All kinds of things appeared and disappeared, including the dinosaurs.

MEASURED IN MILLIONS OF YEARS

Geologists break up Earth's history into ages and periods and give each one a different name. The periods are marked by the kinds of animals and plants that lived at the time. Dinosaurs lived in the Age of Reptiles—the Triassic, Jurassic and Cretaceous periods, between 248 and 65 million years ago.

TIME SPIRAL

If Earth's history is shown as a spiral, with the present-day at the end, it is easy to see that for most of the time only simple kinds of plants and animals existed. About 600 million years ago the first complex animals developed in the sea. The first living things on land appeared about 400 million years ago. Humans did not appear until about 2 million years ago.

FORMATION OF PLANET EARTH
4.6 billion years ago—Earth forms from a mass of swirling space gas and dust.

TRIASSIC-JURASSIC
see pages 16-17

LATE JURASSIC
see pages 18-19

EARLY CRETACEOUS
see pages 20-21

LATE CRETACEOUS
see pages 22-23

END OF THE CRETACEOUS
see pages 24-25

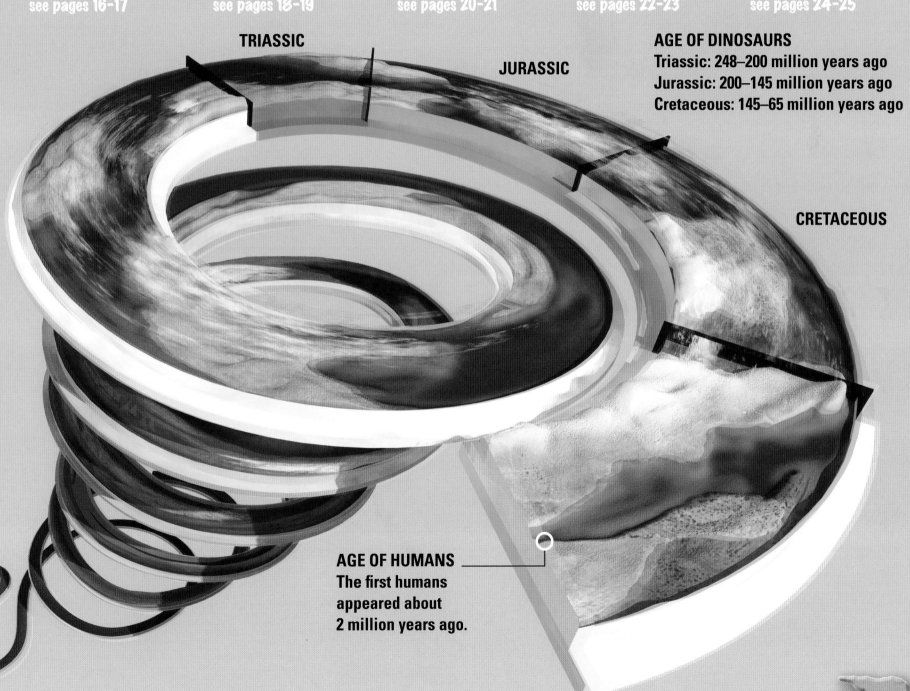

TRIASSIC

JURASSIC

AGE OF DINOSAURS
Triassic: 248–200 million years ago
Jurassic: 200–145 million years ago
Cretaceous: 145–65 million years ago

CRETACEOUS

AGE OF HUMANS
The first humans
appeared about
2 million years ago.

THE DINOSAURS ARRIVE

Late Triassic and Early Jurassic times

About 250 million years ago, hippopotamus-like reptiles chomped the desert plants. They were hunted by land-living crocodiles built like lions. Then came the dinosaurs.

SMALL BEGINNINGS

The animals that came before the dinosaurs were like small crocodiles that ran around on their hind legs. Among the first dinosaurs, the meat-eaters kept the crocodile shape and the two-legged, upright stance. The plant-eaters developed both different shapes and big bodies to allow them to digest their tough food. Some plant-eaters walked on two legs and used them to run away from predators. Other plant-eaters walked on all fours. Some developed armor for protection. As early plant life changed, some plant-eating dinosaurs developed long necks to reach the leaves and twigs on which they fed.

LIFE in the LATE TRIASSIC to EARLY JURASSIC PERIODS

Seas and continents: All the land was joined together as one giant continent known as Pangaea

Climate: Very hot and dry in the middle of the continent; cooler and wetter along the coast

Types of plants: Ferns and conifers

Other large animals: All kinds of reptiles, on land, in the sea and even gliding in the air

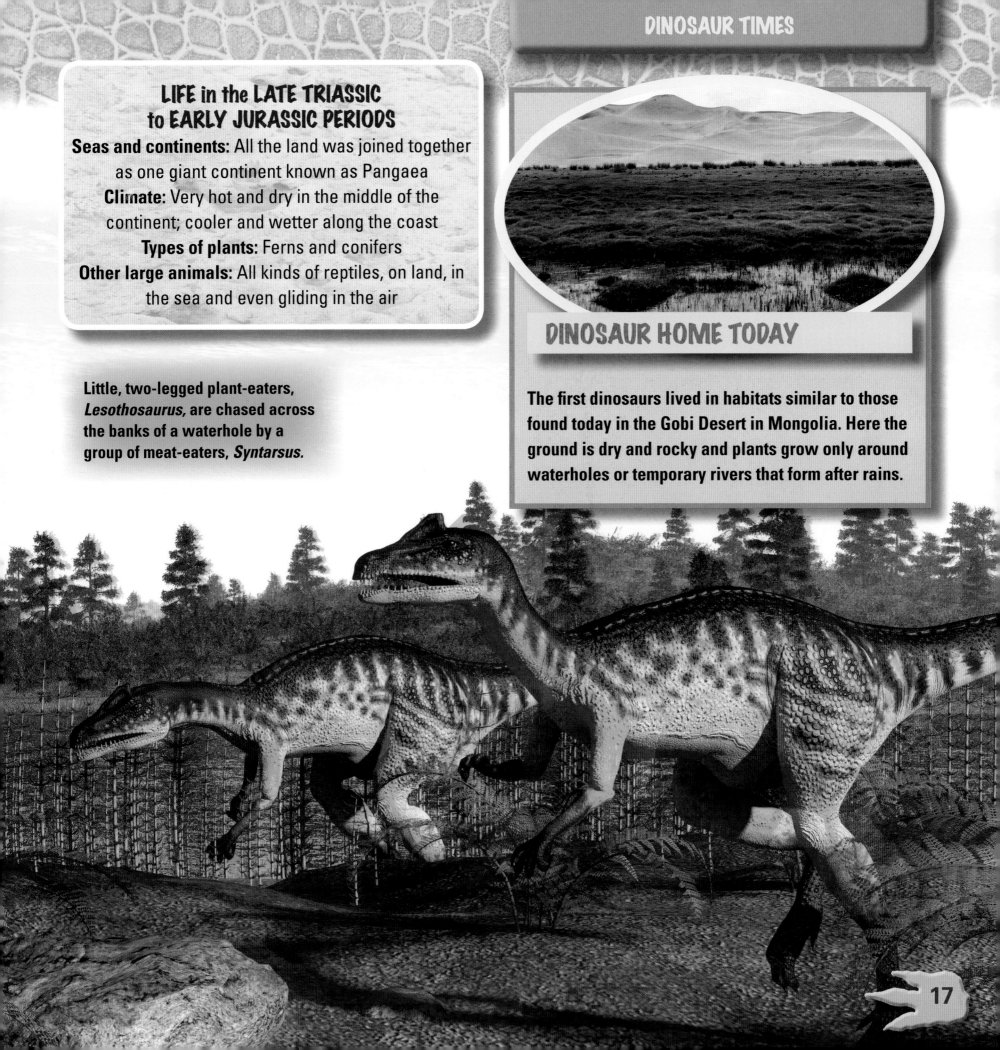

DINOSAUR HOME TODAY

Little, two-legged plant-eaters, *Lesothosaurus,* are chased across the banks of a waterhole by a group of meat-eaters, *Syntarsus.*

The first dinosaurs lived in habitats similar to those found today in the Gobi Desert in Mongolia. Here the ground is dry and rocky and plants grow only around waterholes or temporary rivers that form after rains.

DINOSAURS RULE

Late Jurassic times

By the end of the Jurassic Period, dinosaurs had become the most important group of animals on land.

MILDER CLIMATES

About 160 million years ago the huge continent of Pangaea started to be pulled apart by movements in Earth's surface. Eventually it would split into the continents that exist today. The ocean flowed between the cracks and over low-lying areas. All this water made the climate cooler and moister, which allowed more and newer types of plants to grow.

AT THE HEIGHT OF THE AGE OF DINOSAURS

These new conditions allowed dinosaurs to increase in number and variety. Among plant-eaters, the four-legged, long-necked kinds became more common than the armored and two-legged kinds. Meat-eaters included giants that ate the big plant-eaters and smaller ones that hunted tiny animals in the undergrowth. Dinosaurs ruled the land but there were no dinosaurs in the sky or seas.

FOREST LIFE

The plant life and climate of forests in northern New Zealand today are similar to those dinosaurs must have known 150 million years ago.

LIFE in the LATE JURASSIC PERIOD

Seas and continents: The supercontinent of Pangaea was beginning to break apart

Climate: Moister and cooler than before

Types of plants: Mostly ferns and conifers but now cycads too

Other large animals: Flying and swimming reptiles and the earliest mammals and birds

On the edge of a Late Jurassic forest, a meat-eating *Allosaurus* attacks a plant-eating *Diplodocus*.

SWAMPLANDS

The Okavango Delta in Botswana, a country in southern Africa, is a giant swamp for much of the year. Low-lying land with trees surrounds reed- and lily-filled lakes. This is similar to the habitat of dinosaurs during the Early Cretaceous Period.

A fish-eating *Baryonyx* dashes in among a herd of *Iguanodon* feeding on the reeds of a swamp.

THE AGE OF CHANGE

Early Cretaceous times

By Early Cretaceous times, the giant landmass had broken apart but sea levels remained high, producing widespread swampy areas.

NEW CONTINENTS, NEW ANIMALS

As continents were formed and moved apart, new habitats developed. Dinosaurs and other animals evolved, or changed, to fit the new living areas. Among plant-eating dinosaurs, long-necked kinds gave way to two-legged and armored kinds. Meat-eating dinosaurs got bigger and more varied. In the seas, reptiles such as the plesiosaurs and ichthyosaurs swam. And in the sky, pterosaurs and other reptiles flew. There were many birds in the air, and on the ground early mammals roamed the land. The birds and mammals were mostly small.

LIFE in the EARLY CRETACEOUS PERIOD

Seas and continents: The supercontinent is now broken up into five or six continents

Climate: Generally mild—warm and damp

Types of plants: Unchanged since Jurassic times—ferns, conifers, cycads

Other large animals: Flying and swimming reptiles, birds and mammals

THE LAST DINOSAURS

100 to 65 million years ago

Late Cretaceous times

The continents were now similar to those of today. They provided homes for the widest variety of dinosaurs that ever lived.

A FAMILIAR WORLD

Dinosaurs now lived in habitats like those of today. There was still no grass, but there were forests of conifers and broadleaved trees. In what is now North America, two-legged plant-eating dinosaurs with ducklike bills filled the forests. Herds of horned dinosaurs roamed across the ferny plains. Armored dinosaurs lurked in the undergrowth. Meat-eating dinosaurs were everywhere.

LIFE in the LATE CRETACEOUS PERIOD

Seas and continents: All the continents are separate and are drifting apart

Climate: Mostly warm and moist but cool or dry in places

Types of plants: Flowering plants appear

Other large animals: Many different reptiles, birds and mammals

COVERED IN FORESTS

Most of the last of the dinosaurs spent their lives in or around forests that were similar to those covering much of present-day North America, northern Europe and northern Russia.

An *Albertosaurus*, a fierce meat-eating dinosaur, threatens to attack a herd of *Corythosaurus*—a duckbill dinosaur that fed on ferns and conifers.

23

DINOSAUR EXTINCTION

65 million years ago

The Age of Dinosaurs may have ended violently

What happened to the dinosaurs? Why did they become extinct, or die out?

DEATH FROM THE SKY

Scientists believe that 65 million years ago a giant lump of rock from space crashed into Earth, creating earthquakes and tsunamis, which are giant waves. The explosion burned up the atmosphere, making the air unbreathably hot, and it rained red-hot ash over vast areas.

Gradually, the clouds of smoke and ash blotted out the sun, chilling Earth's surface. Most of the plant life died off, and the plant-eating dinosaurs that survived the initial impact starved. When the plant-eaters died, the meat-eating dinosaurs had nothing to eat and they died off, too. Many other kinds of animals, and many plants, also became extinct.

Eventually the skies cleared, the Earth warmed, and new plants began to grow. By then it was too late for the dinosaurs.

There are other possible reasons for dinosaurs becoming extinct.

Disease
A new kind of germ may have evolved that was particularly deadly to dinosaurs.

Climate change
As continents moved, climates changed, killing off the dinosaurs' food.

Volcanic eruptions
There were big volcanic eruptions at this time. They could have destroyed dinosaur habitats.

Other animals
Mammals may have eaten the dinosaurs' eggs.

EVIDENCE OF A CATASTROPHE

The Meteor Crater in Arizona was formed by a meteorite impact 50,000 years ago. The meteorite that struck Earth at the end of the Cretaceous Period probably created a crater many times deeper and wider.

Following a meteorite strike, many plants and dinosaurs are dying while mouselike early mammals are finding it easier to live. Eventually, the dinosaurs will die out and mammals will become kings of the animal world.

AFTER THE DINOSAURS

New types of animals evolved to fill the world

What happened once the dinosaurs had disappeared? Another group of animals became important and many different kinds of creatures appeared.

MAMMALS ON THE RISE

Mammals had been small in size, number and variety throughout the Age of Dinosaurs. Now it was their turn to become the most dominant animals on Earth.

Wherever there is food available, a creature will develop to eat it. With the dinosaurs gone, some little mammals developed into animals similar to rhinos and elephants to replace the big plant-eating dinosaurs. Meat-eating mammals such as cats and dogs developed to hunt the plant-eaters.

Over time, the world became full of life again. At first there were all kinds of strange animals—those with long legs, short legs, big heads, small heads, long tails, short tails. Over millions of years most of these died out to leave the main mammal groups that are alive today.

THE SURVIVING DINOSAURS

Did any dinosaurs survive? Not exactly, but the smallest of the meat-eating dinosaurs developed into birds during the Late Cretaceous Period. These survived the great extinction 65 million years ago and they are still around. So, perhaps the dinosaurs did not really become extinct, they just grew wings and flew away!

Not everything was killed off at the end of the Cretaceous Period. While dinosaurs became extinct, little mammals and birds survived.

TYRANNOSAURUS

Tie-RAN-o-SAW-rus

Giant hunter of the forests

Tyrannosaurus was one of the fiercest hunters that ever lived. It had a large, powerful body, massive hind legs and strong jaws filled with sharp teeth. It may also have croaked like a bullfrog.

TEARING ITS VICTIM APART

When a *Tyrannosaurus* charged at an animal, the ground shook. The dinosaur kicked up leaves, twigs and dust high into the air.

As a *Tyrannosaurus* got close to its victim, it opened its mouth wide. It swept its great jaws down, tearing off strips of flesh. Its prey fell to the ground in pain and died slowly from shock and loss of blood. Then the *Tyrannosaurus* used its teeth and jaws to crush bones and tear meat from the dead body.

TOP 5

FIVE FIERCEST DINOSAURS

The fiercest dinosaurs were a mixed group

Albertosaurus
Almost as big as *Tyrannosaurus*. Lived in North America 70 mya.

Alioramus
Horse-sized and with a long snout. Lived in China 70 to 65 mya.

Yutyrannus
About 30 feet (9.1 m) long and covered in feathers. Lived in China 125 mya.

Cryolophosaurus
About half the size of *Tyrannosaurus*. Lived in Antarctica when it was warm 185 mya.

Ceratosaurus
Like a dragon, with horns on its nose. Lived in North America 150 mya.

A LONE HUNTER

Tigers are big, fierce meat-eaters that hunt alone in forests like *Tyrannosaurus* did. A tiger waits for an animal to come close and then it moves forward, slowly. Finally it pounces and bites its victim's throat until the animal suffocates.

Tyrannosaurus had a long, deep head with muscular jaws. Its eyes were small. It kept its arms still as it ran.

TYRANNOSAURUS FACT FILE

Meaning of name: "Tyrant lizard"
Length: 40 feet (12.2 m)
Height: 13 feet (4.0 m)
Weight: 6 tons (5.4 tonnes)
Time: Late Cretaceous, 65 mya
Food: Other dinosaurs
Place: North America

A *Carnotaurus* on the hunt. With its sharp teeth it cut deep into its victim's flesh and broke the animal's bones. It may have used its horns for showing off to mates and for head-butting enemies.

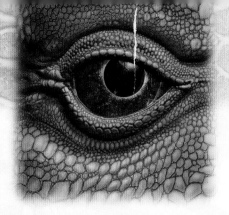

CARNOTAURUS

KAR-no-TAW-rus

The bull-horned hunter of the Southern Hemisphere

CARNOTAURUS FACT FILE

Meaning of name: "Meat-eating bull"

Length: 25 feet (7.6 m)

Height: 11 feet (3.3 m)

Weight: 1.6 tons (1.5 tonnes)

Time: Late Cretaceous, 65 mya

Food: Other dinosaurs

Place: South America

DINO SIZE

Tyrannosaurus lived only in North America. In South America, Carnotaurus took its place as the biggest, fiercest meat-eater.

ANOTHER FEARSOME CREATURE

From a distance, *Carnotaurus* looked like *Tyrannosaurus*—small body on strong hind legs, huge head with toothy jaws, tiny arms. Seen up close, its head was short and narrow, and it had two great horns sticking out, like the horns of a bull. Its arms were just stubs, with the fingers hardly visible.

Carnotaurus had strong legs, showing that it could run fast. The muscles of its neck and its deep skull show that it may have used its head as a club, bringing down its open mouth on the back of its prey to stun it.

VICIOUS HUNTER

While the tiger is the biggest and fiercest meat-eater in India today, the lion is the biggest and fiercest in Africa. Both are like kings but on different continents, as were *Tyrannosaurus* and *Carnotaurus*.

Spinosaurus walked along riverbanks or waded into ponds to catch fish. It also ate other small animals, including little dinosaurs.

SPINOSAURUS FACT FILE

Meaning of name: "Spined lizard"
Length: 48 feet (14.6 m)
Height: 18 feet (5.5 m) including sail
Weight: 7 tons (6.35 tonnes)
Time: 95 mya, start of the Late Cretaceous
Food: Mostly fish
Place: Egypt and Morocco

SPINOSAURUS

SPINE-o-SAW-rus

A fish-eating giant with a tall sail

Spinosaurus ate mostly fish, grabbing them with the sharp claws on its hands. Or it stuck its head into the water and caught fish with its long, thin pointed teeth.

DINO SIZE

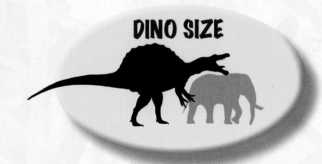

WARMING UP, COOLING DOWN

Spinosaurus had a row of stiff spines along its back, some more than 4 feet (1.2 m) long. Skin stretched between the spines, making a giant sail. Many scientists think the sail helped *Spinosaurus* warm up in cold conditions and cool down in hot weather.

Each morning, the dinosaur held its sail to the sun to warm blood flowing through the sail. When *Spinosaurus* got too hot, it held its sail to the wind. The wind cooled *Spinosaurus*'s blood, lowering its body temperature.

Some scientists believe the sail was brightly colored and was used for display. Perhaps the colors attracted female *Spinosaurus* or made the dinosaur look more fierce.

LARGE AND FIERCE FISH-HUNTER

A Grizzly bear grabs fish from rivers just as *Spinosaurus* did. It also eats other small animals and some insect grubs and plants. Grizzly bears live mostly in forests but *Spinosaurus* lived in forests, deserts and beside rivers.

GIGANOTOSAURUS

JYE-gan-O-toe-SAW-rus

One of the longest meat-eating dinosaurs on Earth

As giant, long-necked plant-eaters evolved in Early Cretaceous South America, so did *Giganotosaurus* to prey on them.

THE SLOW KILLER

Giganotosaurus had steak-knife teeth for slicing food, so it must have killed plant-eaters by shearing the flesh from their bones. Its huge claws on its three-fingered hands were much bigger than those of the other big meat-eating dinosaurs. *Giganotosaurus* used these claws for holding on to struggling prey until they were dead.

GIGANOTOSAURUS FACT FILE

Meaning of name: "Giant lizard from the south"
Length: 43 feet (13 m)
Height: 13 feet (4.0 m)
Weight: 6.5 tons (5.9 tonnes)
Time: 97 mya
Food: Other big dinosaurs
Place: South America

THE WORLD'S LARGEST CARNIVORE

The biggest meat-eating animal on land today is the polar bear. It eats mostly seals and is a very dangerous animal if threatened by people. But at 10 feet (3 m) long, it is tiny compared to the great meat-eating dinosaurs such as *Giganotosaurus*.

With a brain the size of a grapefruit, *Giganotosaurus* was probably not very intelligent.

DEINONYCHUS

die-NON-ee-CUSS

A pack-hunting, birdlike animal

Not all meat-eating dinosaurs were huge. *Deinonychus* **was about the size of a wolf and, like a wolf, it hunted in packs.**

PACK OF DEATH

Deinonychus was covered in feathers like a huge bird of prey. And it was just as fast and vicious. It had a huge, sickle-shaped killing claw on each second toe and it used these to slash its prey to death while holding the animal tightly with its long fingers.

Hunting in packs, *Deinonychus* could bring down much bigger animals than itself. It must have been a scary sight as dozens of the predators with their big, sawlike teeth and powerful talons overpowered their prey and went in for the kill.

HUNTING IN PACKS

Modern animals such as gray wolves, lions and hyenas hunt in packs. Working together, they can follow herds of their prey and then stalk an individual, creep up on it, circle it and attack it from all sides, just as a pack of *Deinonychus* **would have done millions of years ago.**

TOP 5

FIVE SMALL DINOSAURS

Microraptor
The smallest dinosaur known. It was light enough to glide on feathered wings on front and hind legs. Lived in China 160 mya.

Oviraptor
Head like a cassowary, as big as a turkey. Lived in Mongolia 75 mya.

Troodon
Like *Deinonychus* but much slimmer and with smaller killing claws. Lived in North America 70 mya.

Guanlong
Feathery and about the size of an ostrich. Lived in China 160 mya.

Compsognathus
Chicken-sized; one of the smallest of dinosaurs. Lived in Germany and France 150 mya.

DINO SIZE

DEINONYCHUS FACT FILE
Meaning of name: "Terrible claw"
Length: 11 feet (3.4 m)—most of this was tail
Height: 3 feet (0.9 m)
Weight: 160 pounds (72.6 kg)
Time: 110 mya
Food: Bigger dinosaurs than itself
Place: North America

Deinonychus had a small body that was balanced by a long, stiff tail. Standing on one foot, it could slash out with the other.

PLATEOSAURUS
PLAT-ee-o-SAW-rus

A herd-living, gentle giant of the deserts

The long-necked, plant-eating dinosaurs were the biggest land-living animals ever. But the earliest of them were rather small. *Plateosaurus* was about the size of a cow. Even so, it was the biggest animal of its time.

ALWAYS ON THE MOVE

In early dinosaur times, deserts covered most of the continents and plant-life was sparse. Plant-eating animals had to move from one oasis to another to find enough to eat and drink.

Plateosaurus moved across the deserts in herds, walking on all fours or on their hind legs. To feed, they used their rough, saw-edged teeth like a cheesegrater or vegetable slicer to shred the leathery and prickly desert plants. It was a very common animal, and its fossil remains have been found all over Europe.

DINO SIZE

PLATEOSAURUS FACT FILE
Meaning of name: "Broad lizard"
Length: 26 feet (7.9 m)
Height: 7 feet (2.1 m)
Weight: 0.7 tons (635 kg)
Time: 210 mya
Food: Desert plants
Place: Central Europe

A ROUGH DIET

Today, warthogs cross the dusty plains of Africa, eating any tough plants that they can find in the hot, dry climate, just as herds of *Plateosaurus* did.

Plateosaurus sometimes became stuck in quicksand and were overcome by meat-eating dinosaurs and the crocodile-like animals that lived in the desert streams.

Diplodocus wandered across the plains in herds, keeping a constant lookout for predators.

DIPLODOCUS
DIP-loh-DOE-cus

The longest plant-eating dinosaur on Earth

Diplodocus ate like an enormous vacuum cleaner, reaching out and swishing its long neck so that its mouth could take up lots of low-growing plants.

DINO SIZE

THE LONGEST DINOSAUR

Among the long-necked, plant-eaters of the middle of the Age of Dinosaurs, some were tall and reached high up into trees while others were long and short and fed on low-growing plants. *Diplodocus* was the longest of the low-feeding kinds. Its body was as big as an elephant's but its head was only the size of a horse's head. *Diplodocus* would have had to spend most of its time eating to get enough food to survive.

UP AND DOWN

Diplodocus had a finely balanced body. Its great long tail held out at the rear balanced the weight of its long neck. This allowed the dinosaur to reach out far over the ground without falling forward. It was also lightweight enough to rise up on its hind legs and stretch its neck up high into trees. In this way, *Diplodocus* could feed both on wide, open plains and along treelined banks of rivers.

LOW GRAZERS

Modern animals such as kudus that feed from the ground eat mostly grass and the leaves of shrubs. But there were no grass or shrubs when *Diplodocus* was around. The dinosaur ate ferns instead.

DIPLODOCUS FACT FILE

Meaning of name: "Double beam"
Length: 89 feet (27.1 m)
Height: 13 feet (4.0 m)
Weight: 10 tons (9.1 tonnes)
Time: 150 mya
Food: Plants
Place: North America

BRACHIOSAURUS

BRACK-ee-o-SAW-rus

A long-necked feeder among the high trees

TOP 5

TALLEST DINOSAURS

Apatosaurus
Like *Diplodocus* but shorter and heavier. Lived in North America 150 mya.

Amargasaurus
Had a double row of long spines down its neck and a low sail on its back. Lived in South America 130 mya.

Camarasaurus
Like *Brachiosaurus* but smaller and with a bigger head. Lived in North America 150 mya.

Shunosaurus
Had a spiked club on the end of its tail, for defense. Lived in China 170 mya.

Saltasaurus
Back covered with a tight armor of little shields. Lived in South America 70 mya.

Brachiosaurus was built like *Diplodocus* but its front legs were longer and its shoulders higher, allowing it to use its long, flexible neck to raise its head high into trees to feed.

A GIANT EATING-MACHINE

Brachiosaurus used its little jaws and comblike teeth to rake twigs, leaves and seed cones from the tops of trees. It repeatedly raked and swallowed food, leaving no time for chewing.

The food went down the dinosaur's neck and into its stomach in a continuous stream. Inside the stomach, the food was ground up by stones that *Brachiosaurus* swallowed from time to time. Like other big plant-eaters, it needed to eat all the time just to take in enough food to fuel its body.

BRACHIOSAURUS FACT FILE
Meaning of name: "Arm lizard"
Length: 85 feet (25.9 m)
Height: 30 feet (9.1 m)
Weight: 24 tons (21.8 tonnes)
Time: Late Jurassic, 150 mya
Food: Leaves, twigs and cones
Place: North America and Africa

FEEDING AT THE TOP

Since leaves can grow at the tops of trees, some animals have evolved to be able to reach them. In modern times it is the giraffe that feeds in this way. In dinosaur times, it was *Brachiosaurus*.

The tallest animal of the Late Jurassic plains was *Brachiosaurus*. It could have been seen from miles away.

DINO SIZE

Magyarosaurus lived on islands within a sea that covered modern eastern Europe.

MAGYAROSAURUS
mag-YAR-uh-SAW-rus

A small, long-necked plant-eater

Magyarosaurus wasn't much bigger than a cow but its small size helped it survive where there was only a limited amount of food.

MAGYAROSAURUS FACT FILE
Meaning of name: "Magyar lizard"
Length: 20 feet (6.1 m)
Height: 5 feet (1.5 m)
Weight: 1 ton (907 kg)
Time: Late Cretaceous, 70 mya
Food: Island plants **Place:** Romania in Europe

DINO SIZE

ISLAND-DWELLER

In late dinosaur times, there was a chain of islands in what is now eastern Europe. Some of the dinosaurs that lived there were dwarf versions of the animals that lived on the mainland. *Magyarosaurus* was one of these. Its small size gave it the best chance of living on the little food that was available.

ARMOR-BACKED

Some of the later long-necked plant-eaters had armor across their backs. This may have been to protect them from meat-eaters or to help to support their weight. In South America these dinosaurs became the biggest land-living animals ever, but in Europe there were smaller versions, like *Magyarosaurus*.

AN ISLAND MINIATURE

The Shetland pony, native to the islands off the coast of Scotland, is a dwarf horse. *Magyarosaurus* was a dwarf dinosaur.

STEGOSAURUS
STEG-o-SAW-rus

Heavily decorated with plates and a defensive tail

DINO SIZE

TOP 5

OTHER ARMORED DINOSAURS

Scutellosaurus
Small, lizardlike and with a back covered in little shields. Lived in North America 195 mya.

Kentrosaurus
Like a small *Stegosaurus* but with narrow plates and spikes along its tail. Lived in East Africa 150 mya.

Polacanthus
Had plates on the tail, spikes on the back and a shield over the hips. Lived in England 130 mya.

Edmontonia
Had a pavement of armor on its back and spikes around its shoulders. Lived in North America 70 mya.

Styracosaurus
Huge spikes stuck out of an armored neck frill. It also had a nose horn. Lived in North America 70 mya.

Spikes, plates, horns, shields—many of the plant-eating dinosaurs had strong armor to defend themselves against the powerful teeth and claws of the meat-eaters.

PLATES AND SPINES

With its double row of plates sticking up along its back and its heavy, swishing tail with spikes on the end, *Stegosaurus* was one of the most recognizable of all dinosaurs. Scientists used to think that the plates were used as armor to protect the spine. Now experts think that the plates were covered in brightly colored skin and were used to signal other *Stegosaurus*. For sure, the spikes on the tail were used for defense. Swung sideways against the legs and flanks of an attacking meat-eating dinosaur, they would have caused terrible damage.

SMALLER THAN IT LOOKS

When the frilled lizard of Australia is startled, it sticks out its neck flaps, making the animal look bigger and fiercer than it is. *Stegosaurus* may have used its plates in the same way.

Stegosaurus fed from low-growing plants. Sometimes it would rear up on its hind legs to reach leaves on low branches.

STEGOSAURUS FACT FILE
Meaning of name: "Roofed lizard"
Length: 30 feet (9.1 m)
Height: 13 feet (4.0 m)
Weight: 2.5 tons (2.3 tonnes)
Time: Late Jurassic, 150 mya
Food: Plants
Place: North America

47

Euoplocephalus (below right) shared the forests with another armored dinosaur, *Edmontonia* (below left). Instead of a club on the tail for defense, *Edmontonia* had spikes on the shoulders.

DINO SIZE

EUOPLOCEPHALUS
YOU-oh-plo-SEF-ah-lus

Solid defense against the fiercest dinosaurs of the time

EUOPLOCEPHALUS FACT FILE

Meaning of name: "Well-armored head"
Length: 20 feet (6.1 m)
Height: 5 feet (1.5 m)
Weight: 2.2 tons (2 tonnes)
Time: Late Cretaceous, 70 mya
Food: Low-growing plants
Place: North America

Four powerful legs spread wide apart were needed to support the great weight of armor on this animal's back. *Euoplocephalus* was the most heavily armored dinosaur of them all.

A LIVING TANK

Nothing, not even the biggest meat-eating dinosaurs, could get through the armor of *Euoplocephalus*. Its head and back were covered in armor as was its tail down to the heavy club on the end. Even its eyelids were covered in armor and they could be slammed shut like the shutters of a tank when danger approaches.

The tail club of *Euoplocephalus* was solid bone, and the tail itself was stiff and straight. The tail could be swung sideways to deliver a blow that would smash the legs of any dinosaur that attacked. But *Euoplocephalus* was a gentle animal that spent most of its time munching low-growing flowering plants.

COVERED IN ARMOR

Nothing alive today is as heavily armored as *Euoplocephalus* was. The closest is the armadillo, which has an armored head, body and tail. A giant armadillo is only one-fifth the size of *Euoplocephalus* but today's fierce meat-eaters are themselves much smaller than the great tyrannosaurs of the past.

STYGIMOLOCH

STIH-jee-MAWL-uk

Two rivals batter it out

A group of plant-eating dinosaurs that scientists call "the boneheads" had a massive lump of bone on top of the head, and most had horns and knobs, too. *Stygimoloch* was the weirdest of these creatures.

HEAD-BANGING

Stygimoloch used its bony head as a battering ram. It would charge full-force into the flanks of an enemy, its skull and neck absorbing the impact. The dinosaur also had a remarkable arrangement of horns on the snout and around the back of the skull. It may have used these as weapons in fighting but they would certainly have helped to make the animal look really frightening.

STYGIMOLOCH FACT FILE

Meaning of name: "Horned demon from the river of death"
Length: 10 feet (3 m)
Height at hips: 3 feet (0.9 m)
Weight: 200 pounds (90.7 kg)
Time: Late Cretaceous, 70 mya
Food: Plants
Place: North America

KNOCKING HEADS TOGETHER

Nowadays, deer, bison, rhinos and giraffes use their horns for fighting one another. Bighorn rams crash their heavy heads together when they compete for leadership of the flock. In dinosaur times, *Stygimoloch* would have done the same.

As well as fighting enemies and meat-eating dinosaurs, *Stygimoloch* males would fight among themselves for leadership of the herd.

The sheer size of *Triceratops*, along with its three horns, made it distinctive from the other horned dinosaurs of the time.

TRICERATOPS
tri-SAIR-uh-tops

Three-horned feeding machine

As herds of horned dinosaurs roamed the plains, these animals recognized their own kind by the different arrangements of horns and frills that they carried.

PROTECTING ITS YOUNG

The biggest of the horned dinosaurs was *Triceratops.* It had a rhinoceros-like body and a massive head with a huge, armored shield around the neck. On top of its head were two long horns pointing forward from above the eyes, and on its nose was a smaller horn.

Triceratops moved about in herds, always looking for plants to eat. For protection, large adults would have led a herd with the young keeping close to their parents. If a herd was attacked by a giant meat-eater such as a *Tyrannosaurus,* the adult *Triceratops* probably gathered round the little ones and pointed their horns outward in defense.

HORNED FOR PROTECTION

The closest living animal to *Triceratops* is the rhinoceros, with its big body and defensive horn. It will fight hard to protect its young.

DINO SIZE

TRICERATOPS FACT FILE
Meaning of name: "Three-horned head"
Length: 30 feet (9.1 m) **Height:** 6 feet (1.8 m)
Weight: 6.5 tons (5.9 tonnes)
Time: Late Cretaceous, 65 mya
Food: Low-growing plants
Place: North America

HETERODONTOSAURUS

HET-ur-o-DON-toh-SAW-rus

A dinosaur with tusks, teeth and a beak

Dinosaurs are usually thought of as being huge, scary beasts but some two-footed, plant-eating kinds such as *Heterodontosaurus* were rather small. Many were the size of goats, living among the feet of the giants.

DIFFERENT TEETH

Heterodontosaurus had a strange set of teeth for such a little animal. At the front of its mouth, on the upper jaw, were chopping teeth. These worked against a beak on the lower jaw and were used for gathering food. Farther back was a pair of tusks that may have been used to dig up roots or, among male *Heterodontosaurus*, to display to one another. At the back of the mouth were chopping and grinding teeth, used for chewing plant food.

Apart from its teeth, *Heterodontosaurus* was much like other small plant-eating dinosaurs. It had a heavy body supported on two strong hind legs and balanced by a heavy tail. The front legs were small and the hands had four or five fingers.

DINO SIZE

HETERODONTOSAURUS FACT FILE

Meaning of name: "Lizard with different types of teeth"
Length: 3 feet (0.9 m)
Height: 1 foot (30 cm)
Weight: 5 pounds (2.3 kg)
Time: Early Jurassic, 195 mya
Food: Plants
Place: South Africa

Modern gazelles use their strong hind legs to run away from meat-eating animals such as lions and cheetahs. *Heterodontosaurus* may have escaped predators using its strong hind legs in the same way.

BOUNCING OUT OF TROUBLE

The different types of teeth allowed *Heterodontosaurus* to eat whatever food it could find on the dusty plains.

IGUANODON
ih-GWAN-o-dahn

A dinosaur that prowled swamps and wetlands

TOP 5

WATER-LOVING DINOSAURS

Ouranosaurus
Like *Iguanodon* but with a sail on its back. Lived in Africa 120 mya.

Parasaurolophus
With a ducklike beak and a huge, curved crest on its head. Lived in North America 60 mya.

Tsintaosaurus
Like *Parasaurolophus* but with the crest upright like a unicorn's horn. Lived in China 60 mya.

Hypsilophodon
Probably the fastest of the small, two-footed plant-eaters. Lived in England 135 mya.

Tenontosaurus
Like a medium-sized *Iguanodon* but with an extremely long tail. Lived in North America 110 mya.

Iguanodon was one of the first dinosaurs to be discovered, almost 200 years ago.

FEEDING LOW, FEEDING HIGH

Iguanodon moved around mostly on all fours, rising on its hind legs only when it wanted to reach food from the low branches of trees. It had very strange hands. The three middle fingers were strong and equipped with hoofs, bearing the animal's weight as it walked on all fours. The thumbs were big, horny spikes used for defense and for pulling down branches of trees. The little finger of each hand was very flexible and was used for grasping.

IGUANODON FACT FILE
Meaning of name: "Iguana toothed"
Length: 33 feet (10.1 m)
Height: 15 feet (4.6 m)
Weight: 2.5 tons (2.3 tonnes)
Time: Early Cretaceous, 135 mya
Food: Plants
Place: England and Belgium

DINO SIZE

SWAMP-FEEDING GIANT

A hippopotamus uses its lips to grab clumps of grass to eat. An *Iguanodon* probably used the horny beak at the front of its jaws in much the same way.

Iguanodon may have moved about in herds across the marshy lands of northern Europe.

Unlike many of the duckbilled dinosaurs, *Edmontosaurus* had a flat head with no crest of any kind. It had scaly skin.

EDMONTOSAURUS
ed-MON-toh-SAW-rus

A giant with the mouth of a duck

EDMONTOSAURUS FACT FILE
Meaning of name: "Lizard from Edmonton"
Length: 43 feet (13.1 m)
Height when on hind legs: 15 feet (4.6 m)
Weight: 4.4 tons (4 tonnes)
Time: Late Cretaceous, 65 mya
Food: Tough vegetation
Place: North America

DINO SIZE

The duckbills were the most common of the plant-eaters at the end of the Age of Dinosaurs. They roamed in herds across North America and Asia. *Edmontosaurus* was the commonest of these dinosaurs.

MIGRATING MASSES

Edmontosaurus was as big as a school bus, with hind legs heavier than the front legs and with a big, flat-sided tail. It walked mostly on all fours but it could rear up on its hind legs to feed. Its neck was very flexible, allowing it to gather plants in awkward corners, and its mouth was broad and flat with a ducklike bill, or beak. *Edmontosaurus* used its bill for scraping leaves and twigs from the trees.

Fossil evidence shows that herds of *Edmontosaurus* roamed along beaches and through salty marshes. In the nesting seasons, the herds gathered and brought up their young together.

LIVING IN SALTY CONDITIONS

Today there are many animals that live, feed and nest in salty marshes as *Edmontosaurus* did. Flamingos, for example, nest together in huge flocks in nests made from heaps of mud and twigs.

OLOROTITAN

OH-lo-roh-TIGHT-un

A colorful, crested show-off

Enormous body, big hind legs, small front legs, massive tail, beak like a duck's—it must be a duckbill dinosaur. But one thing made it really stand out.

HONK IF YOU'RE AN OLOROTITAN!

Olorotitan was one of the last of the two-legged, plant-eating dinosaurs in the Northern Hemisphere. Its unique head crest set it apart from the many other duckbills around at the time. Some duckbill crests were long and curved, some were semicircular and others stuck up like a Mohawk. *Olorotitan* had a crest that was swept back and expanded like the blade of an ax.

A duckbill's crest was made up of bones of the nose, and many of the bones were hollow. The dinosaur may have used the crest as a musical instrument, to honk signals to one another through the forests and across the plains. But the crest's main job was to act like a flag or signal.

OLOROTITAN FACT FILE

Meaning of name: "Giant swan"
Length: 39 feet (11.9 m) long
Height: 11 feet (3.4 m) long
Weight: 4.4 tons (4 tonnes)
Time: Late Cretaceous, 65 mya
Food: Tough plants
Place: Eastern Russia

DINO SIZE

LOOK AT ME!

The modern hornbill has a big crest on its head, made up of part of the beak. Its bright coloring makes it easy to see. Like the crest of some of the duckbills, the hornbill's crest is used for showing off.

An *Olorotitan* returns to its nest to check that predators have not taken its eggs. It will signal to others at any sign of danger.

FOSSIL FINDS

Uncovering clues and evidence of the past

Remains of dinosaurs are embedded in rocks but paleontologists—scientists who study fossils—have to know where to find them.

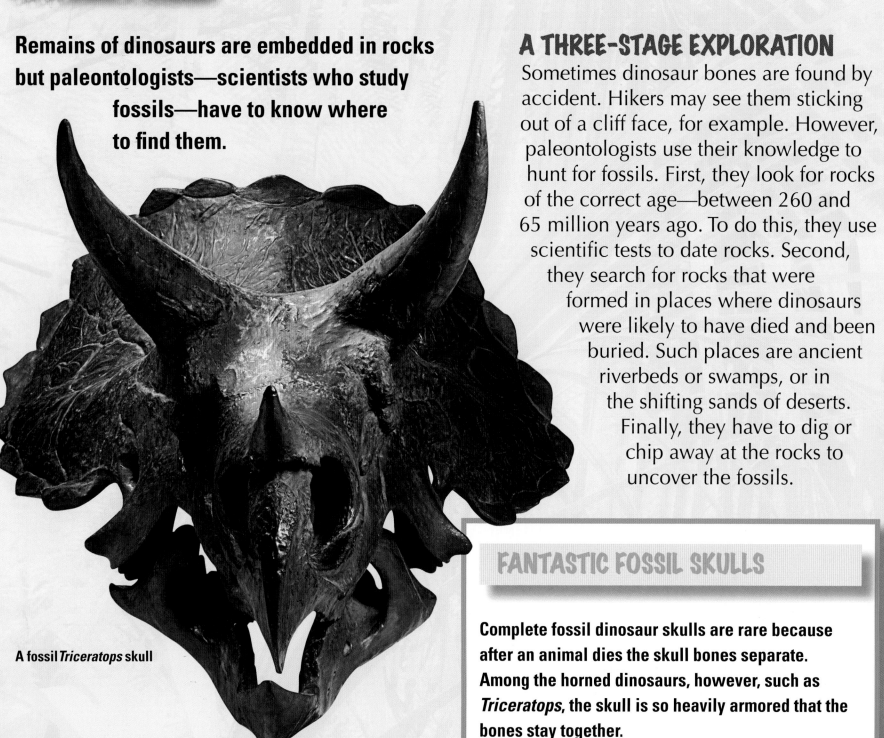

A fossil *Triceratops* skull

A THREE-STAGE EXPLORATION

Sometimes dinosaur bones are found by accident. Hikers may see them sticking out of a cliff face, for example. However, paleontologists use their knowledge to hunt for fossils. First, they look for rocks of the correct age—between 260 and 65 million years ago. To do this, they use scientific tests to date rocks. Second, they search for rocks that were formed in places where dinosaurs were likely to have died and been buried. Such places are ancient riverbeds or swamps, or in the shifting sands of deserts. Finally, they have to dig or chip away at the rocks to uncover the fossils.

FANTASTIC FOSSIL SKULLS

Complete fossil dinosaur skulls are rare because after an animal dies the skull bones separate. Among the horned dinosaurs, however, such as *Triceratops*, the skull is so heavily armored that the bones stay together.

EXTRAORDINARY FINDS

Paleontologists sometimes find a whole dinosaur skeleton, with its bones joined to one another just as they would have been when the animal was alive.

63

As small, scavenging dinosaurs pick clean the skeleton of a dead *Triceratops* they leave their footprints in the sand. If shifting sand dunes cover the skeleton, bones and footprints may eventually be fossilized.

FOSSILIZATION

How fossil bones have formed

Fossils are not actual dead flesh and bones but are rock material that replaced them. There are a number of ways in which once-living material turned to stone.

FOSSIL BONES AS EXAMPLES

Bone can rot away leaving a hole in rock material. The hole may be filled with minerals dissolved in water that trickles through the material. As the minerals dry and harden, they form a lump in the shape of the bone. Bone material can also be replaced by minerals gradually, molecule by molecule. In this way, the tiny structure of the bone is preserved.

Often bones are crushed flat by the weight of rock material above them so only their outlines are preserved as fossils.

Fossil skull of *Tyrannosaurus*

A dead dinosaur that fell into a lake would not have rotted away. Its remains will be complete.

COMPLETE DINOSAURS

TOP 5 FOSSIL SITES

Dinosaur Provincial Park, Canada
Herds of horned dinosaurs washed away in a flood while crossing a river are fossilized in the riverbed.

Solnhofen, Germany
Limestone rocks from an ancient lagoon contain fossils of little dinosaurs, pterosaurs and the first birds.

Gobi Desert, Mongolia
The fossils of horned dinosaurs, meat-eating dinosaurs and dinosaur eggs and nests have been found in fossilized sand dunes.

Dinosaur National Monument, Utah
Big, meat-eating dinosaurs and huge plant-eating dinosaurs are preserved in river sandstones.

Liaoning, China
Rocks from ancient lake beds hold skeletons of part-dinosaur, part-bird animals.

INTERPRETING THE FINDS

Putting meat, flesh and skin on the bones

Putting meat, flesh and skin on the bones

Take a look at this complete fossil skeleton of a _Chasmosaurus_, a horned dinosaur, and then follow how paleontologists build up a picture of how the animal looked in real life.

BUILDING THE KNOWLEDGE

Incredibly, the only evidence that exists of many dinosaurs is a single bone. By comparing this bone with similar ones from other dinosaurs and prehistoric creatures, and from living animals, it is possible to rebuild or reconstruct the complete skeleton. The shape and size of the skeleton tells a lot about the body systems and how they worked.

FRILLED AND HORNED—
TRICERATOPS
The skull had a huge frill around the rear edge. This would have made the head bigger and more impressive. Horns would have allowed the dinosaur to defend itself.

PIECING EVERYTHING TOGETHER

On these two pages are featured seven key parts of the _Chasmosaurus_ skeleton and alongside each is an example from earlier in the book of a dinosaur that has been reconstructed from similar evidence. Each fragment of evidence about a dinosaur is like a piece of a jigsaw. By fitting the pieces together, paleontologists complete the picture of the animal.

BEAKED AND TOOTHED—_IGUANODON_
The beak shows that the dinosaur could pluck plants. The teeth were arranged to shear past one another like scissors, chopping up tough plant food.

FRONT LEGS—*DEINONYCHUS*
The front legs were shorter than the hind legs. They allowed the dinosaur to turn quickly to face enemies.

LARGE RIB CAGE—
MAGYAROSAURUS
The curve of the ribs shows that the dinosaur had a big body. This would have held a huge stomach able to break down tough plants.

BALANCING TAIL—
CARNOTAURUS
A heavy tail that could swing from side to side would balance the weight of a heavy head and allow the dinosaur to run fast.

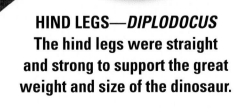

HIND LEGS—*DIPLODOCUS*
The hind legs were straight and strong to support the great weight and size of the dinosaur.

FEET AND TOES—*OLOROTITAN*
Big, broad feet and thick toe bones show the dinosaur had a rhinoceros-sized body yet could run fast.

A restoration of a *Gigantoraptor*, a feathered dinosaur. The colors of the feathers and skin are the artist's idea of how they looked.

RECONSTRUCTIONS

Bringing dinosaurs alive in museums, art and movies

Building a dinosaur skeleton for a museum exhibit is called a reconstruction. Creating a painting or a movie that shows what the complete animal was like is called a restoration. Together they help form a picture of a dinosaur.

MAKING THEM LIVE

To make a dinosaur, the skeleton needs to be dressed—first muscles must be added, then the internal organs and finally the skin.

The size and weight of muscles can be worked out from marks where muscles were attached to the fossil bones. The size and position of organs can be imagined from spaces within and around bones such as the ribs and hips. Whether the skin was leathery or scaly, and if it had feathers, can be revealed from impressions of dinosaurs' skins in rocks.

Some museums display full-sized reconstructions of the big dinosaurs. They even have the dinosaurs mechanically controlled so that they move and roar.

GREAT MUSEUM DISPLAYS

American Museum of Natural History, New York
Some of the most famous of all reconstructed skeletons are here. Many of the dinosaur fossils were found in the western United States more than 100 years ago.

Royal Tyrrell Museum, Drumheller, Canada
A display of the vast dinosaur discoveries of Canada.

The Field Museum, Chicago
Displays include the biggest and most complete *Tyrannosaurus* skeleton ever found.

Museum of the Rockies
One of the world's finest collections of dinosaur skeletons, including several *Triceratops*.

Zigong Dinosaur Museum, Zigong, China
The world's biggest dinosaur museum.

THE BONE-HUNTERS

Early discoveries in Britain and the USA

TOP 5

The first dinosaur discoveries were made in England almost 200 years ago. Dinosaur fever then moved to North America as great fossil finds were made by pioneers heading west to California.

ON THE FOSSIL TRAIL

The first dinosaur found in the United States was a duckbill, a *Hadrosaurus*, in New Jersey in 1858. After the Civil War in 1865, museums and universities organized expeditions to collect dinosaur fossils. A fierce rivalry between paleontologists led to more than 150 kinds of dinosaur being found before 1900. Since then, dinosaur hunters all over the world have unearthed fossils of more than another 450 kinds and new ones are being discovered each year.

WILLIAM BUCKLAND
The first dinosaur bones were found near Oxford in England in 1815 but it was not until 1824 that they were scientifically identified by Buckland. He named the big meat-eater *Megalosaurus*.

MARY ANNING
British fossil collector Mary Anning was studying dinosaur fossils before anybody knew what they were. Her work in the 1820s and 1830s shaped ideas of prehistoric life.

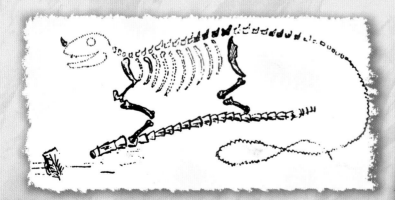

In the 1820s, English country doctor Gideon Mantel made this restoration of an *Iguanodon* skeleton.

EARLY FOSSIL HUNTERS

Othniel Charles Marsh
While Professor of Paleontology at Yale University in the 1890s, he found bones of *Stegosaurus* and *Allosaurus*.

Barnum Brown
In 1902, working for the American Museum of Natural History, he found the first skeleton of *Tyrannosaurus*.

Earl Douglas
Working for the Carnegie Museum in Pittsburgh, he found an almost complete skeleton of *Diplodocus* in 1909.

Friedrich von Heune
In the early 1900s, von Heune from Germany discovered more dinosaurs in Europe than anyone else.

Roy Chapman Andrews
On American Museum of Natural History expeditions to Mongolia in the 1930s, he found the horned *Protoceratops* and the first dinosaur eggs.

Early dinosaur hunters in the United States went on their expeditions fully armed, to deal with rival fossil hunters. The competition between teams of fossil hunters became known as the "bone wars."

WHAT NEXT?

The dinosaur legacy lives on

Just about every month a new dinosaur is discovered and scientists come up with a new theory that changes our views of how dinosaurs looked and lived.

NEW INFORMATION ALL THE TIME

Only since fossil finds in China in 1996 has there been proof that the small meat-eating dinosaurs were covered in feathers. Looking again at a horned dinosaur skeleton that had been in a museum basement for 50 years has just revealed a new kind of dinosaur. And scientists have just found that the math they used to estimate a dinosaur's weight was incorrect. These are changes that make the study of dinosaurs so exciting.

TOP 5

NEW DINOSAURS

Falcarius
Discovered in Utah in 2005. A plant-eater with meat-eater features.

Brachytrachelopan
Discovered in Argentina in 2005. A kind of long-necked plant-eater that actually had a short neck.

Miragaia
Discovered in Portugal in 2009. A plated dinosaur like *Stegosaurus* but it had a long neck.

Linhenykus
Discovered in China in 2011. The latest member found of a group of rabbit-sized meat-eaters that had tiny arms, each with a single enormous claw.

Yutyrannus
Discovered in China in 2012. The biggest feather-covered, meat-eating dinosaur known.

MISTAKEN IDENTITY

In the 1930s, the fossil skeleton of a meat-eating dinosaur *Oviraptor* was found near a dinosaur nest like this one. Paleontologists thought that *Oviraptor* had been raiding the nest. Sixty years later another find showed that the nest actually belonged to an *Oviraptor*.

This is a *Therizinosaurus,* a dinosaur with feathers that was built like a meat-eater but probably ate plants.

QUESTIONS AND ANSWERS

How many dinosaurs were there?

Paleontologists know of a little over 600 kinds but they think that there may be another 1,000 different dinosaurs waiting to be discovered.

How long did they live?

The dinosaurs existed from Late Triassic times until the end of the Cretaceous Period. That is about 160 million years. Compare that with humans who have been on Earth for only the past two million years or so.

What does the word "dinosaur" mean?

The word is made up of two Greek words—*deinos* meaning "terrible" and *sauros* meaning "lizard." It comes from the term *Dinosauria,* a word invented by British scientist Sir Richard Owen in 1842 to describe the three kinds of dinosaur fossils that had been found and studied up to that time.

How smart were dinosaurs?

Some people think that dinosaurs were all slow, stupid animals. Others believe that some of them, especially the small meat-eaters, were as smart as some of today's birds. A turkey-sized meat-eater, *Troodon,* had the biggest brain of any dinosaur known.

Which dinosaurs do scientists know most about?

Most fossil dinosaur skeletons are of individuals that lived close to rivers and lakes or in sandy deserts as in these places an animal's body is easily covered and preserved when it dies. Scientists know almost nothing about any dinosaurs that lived on mountains. Mountain animals hardly ever become buried and so are rarely found as fossils.

What color were dinosaurs?

The fossils of small feathered dinosaurs show microscopic structures similar to those that create the colors of modern bird feathers. From these it seems that the feathers of one dinosaur were black and those of another were orange with black stripes.

Could dinosaurs fly?

Pterosaurs were flying reptiles that lived at the same time as the dinosaurs. They had small, furry bodies and could fly by flapping their broad, leathery wings attached to the arms. The pterosaurs were distantly related to the dinosaurs. The smallest known dinosaur, *Microraptor,* had birdlike flight feathers on its arms and its legs. It was able to glide from tree to tree, but it could not have flapped its wings as in true flight. There is no direct evidence that dinosaurs could fly.

Why do dinosaurs have such long names?

When scientists from many countries get together to talk about an animal, they must give it a name that everybody can understand. They use a Latin or ancient Greek name that has two parts. The first part is given to a collection of animals that look the same, for example *Tyrannosaurus* or *Triceratops.* The second part defines each particular animal of that kind, for instance *rex,* a *Tyrannosaurus,* and *prorsus,* a *Triceratops.* So a dinosaur's complete name would be *Tyrannosaurus rex.* In this book we have used only the first part of the scientific name.

Which dinosaur had the longest horns?

This would be the three-horned *Triceratops.* The bony cores of the eye horns were more than 3 feet (0.9 m) long but they were covered with a pointed horny sheath that would have made them much longer.

Were dinosaurs cold-blooded like reptiles or warm-blooded like birds?

The small meat-eaters were covered in feathers and these would have helped to control the temperature of a warm-blooded animal. The big, long-necked, plant-eaters lacked feathers and their bodies could store body heat as cold-blooded animals do. The bodies of other dinosaurs may have worked as a mix of cold- and warm-blooded.

Which museum has the most kinds of dinosaur?

The American Museum of Natural History in New York has at least 100 different kinds of dinosaurs in its collection.

GLOSSARY

Armor A covering that protects the body.

Barren Having nothing growing on it, as in a desert.

Beak A horny mouth structure of birds and some dinosaurs; also known as a bill.

Blood The fluid that carries life-giving oxygen round the body, refreshed by the lungs and pumped by the heart.

Brain The organ inside the head that controls the nervous system and where all thinking is done.

Climate The average weather conditions—temperature, rainfall and winds— for a particular area.

Cone A fruit-like structure, typically on conifer trees, which has seeds attached to tough scales.

Conifer A tree that carries its seeds in cones; it has needlelike leaves that stay on the tree all year.

Continent A big landmass.

Crater A dish-shaped depression in the ground, formed by a meteorite strike or an exploded volcano.

Crest A structure on an animal's head or back, usually for display.

Cretaceous The period of geological time from 145 million to 65 million years ago.

Cycads Plants with a stout trunk and a bunch of palmlike leaves.

Desert A dry, rocky or sandy area in which very little can grow.

Digest To break down food material into a form that can be used by the body.

Digestive system That part of an animal's body—stomach, liver and intestines—that processes its food.

Dropping Food waste that has passed through an animal's body, with all the nutrients taken out of it.

Duckbill A kind of two-footed, plant-eating dinosaur that had a flat beak like that of a duck.

Environment The living conditions of an animal including the climate and the plants and other animals that live in the area.

Extinct Completely died out.

Fern A nonflowering plant with broad, finely divided leaves known as fronds.

Flexible Able to bend easily.

Flower The part of some plants that produces fruit and seeds.

Fossil The remains of a once-living thing or its parts found preserved in ancient rocks and studied by paleontologists and geologists.

Geological time A measure of the age of Earth and all the changes to its rocks that have happened since it was first formed.

Graze To feed from low-growing plants such as grass.

Horn A structure on the head of an animal that usually has a bony core and a covering of tough material.

Impression Any mark or print in rock made by something pressing in it.

Jurassic The period of geological time from 200 million to 145 million years ago.

Kidneys The organ in the body that removes waste material from the blood and purifies it.

Liver The organ in the body that produces chemicals allowing the digestive system to work.

Lungs The organs in the body that take oxygen from air and deliver it to the blood and get rid of unwanted carbon dioxide.

Mammal Any backboned animal that gives birth to live young and feeds them on milk. It includes lions, wolves, rats, monkeys and humans.

Marsh A swampy area, usually near the sea and with salty water.

Mineral A chemical substance that is a building block of rocks.

Muscle Part of an animal's body that allows it to move by pulling on bones or to squeeze material such as food in the stomach.

Oasis A fertile area in a desert, with water to drink.

Ocean A vast area of seawater; the opposite of a continent.

Offspring The young of an animal.

Paleontologist A person who studies ancient living things by examining fossils.

Pangaea The supercontinent that included all the landmasses of the world between about 400 million and 200 million years ago.

Plain A large, open area of flat land, usually covered in low-growing plants such as grass. Known in North America as a prairie.

Predator Any animal that hunts and kills other animals to eat.

Prey Any animal that is hunted and eaten by another.

Quicksand Soft sand in which an animal can become trapped and sink.

Reptile A cold-blooded animal that lays hard-shelled or leathery eggs on land. Modern reptiles include snakes, crocodiles, turtles and lizards.

Sail On an animal, a large crest on the back formed of skin stretched over long, bony structures.

Shield A broad piece of armor.

Spike A pointed structure used as a weapon.

Swamp An area of waterlogged land.

Tendon A kind of natural cable in the body that joins muscles to bones.

Triassic The period of geological time from 248 million to 200 million years ago.

Tsunami A huge destructive sea wave, usually produced by an underwater earthquake.

Undergrowth The plants that grow on the ground below the trees in a forest.

Volcano An opening on Earth's surface through which hot, molten rock, ash and gas burst from deep inside, often building up to form a mountain.

FINDING OUT MORE

BOOKS

Dixon, Dougal. *Amazing Dinosaurs.* Honesdale, P.A.: Boyds Mills Press, 2007.

Haines, Tim, and Paul Chambers. *The Complete Guide to Prehistoric Life.* Buffalo, N.Y.: Firefly Books (U.S.), 2006.

Holtz, Thomas R., and Luis V. Rey. *Dinosaurs: The Most Complete, Up-to-Date Encyclopedia for Dinosaur Lovers of All Ages.* New York: Random House, 2007.

Lessem, Don, and Franco Tempesta. *The Ultimate Dinopedia: The Most Complete Dinosaur Reference Ever.* Washington, D.C.: National Geographic, 2010.

Switek, Brian. *My Beloved Brontosaurus: On the Road with Old Bones, New Science, and Our Favorite Dinosaurs.* New York: Scientific American/Farrar, Straus and Giroux, 2013.

WEBSITES

Test your knowledge about dinosaurs:
http://kids.nationalgeographic. com/kids/games/puzzlesquizzes/ brainteaserdinosaurs/

The Smithsonian Museum of Natural History dinosaur site:
http://paleobiology.si.edu/dinosaurs/

Play dinosaur games and read all about dinosaurs:
http://www.kidsdinos.com/

The Evolving Planet exhibition at the Field Museum in Chicago fits dinosaurs into Earth's living history:
http://fieldmuseum.org/happening/ exhibits/evolving-planet

Visit the fossil halls at the American Museum of Natural History in New York City:
http://www.amnh.org/exhibitions/ permanent-exhibitions/fossil-halls/

INDEX